Canada

Jabberwocky Books
2301 Lucien Way #415
Maitland, FL 32751
407.339.4217
www.jabberwocky-books.com

Jabberwocky
Books

Printed in the United States of America.

ISBN-13: 978-1-54566-559-6

ABCDetroit

Enzo,
Happy Birthday &
Happy Reading!
-♡-
Christopher

Written by Kari Jo Wagner
Illustrated by Aprilia Muktirina

JABBERWOCKY BOOKS

At the **museum of A**frican American history, open in 1965, celebrate black culture and see history come alive.

Spend a day on beautiful **B**elle Isle, see the aquarium or nature museum and stay awhile.

Coney dogs! Can you eat just one?
Chili sauce, onions and mustard on a bun.

Freighters on the **D**etroit River haul cargo,
tons of cement and sand from the Atlantic to Chicago.

Eastern Market has fresh foods, flowers and more.
Treat yourself on this large historic market floor.

In Detroit, **F**ord invented the assembly line, helping make Model Ts in record time.

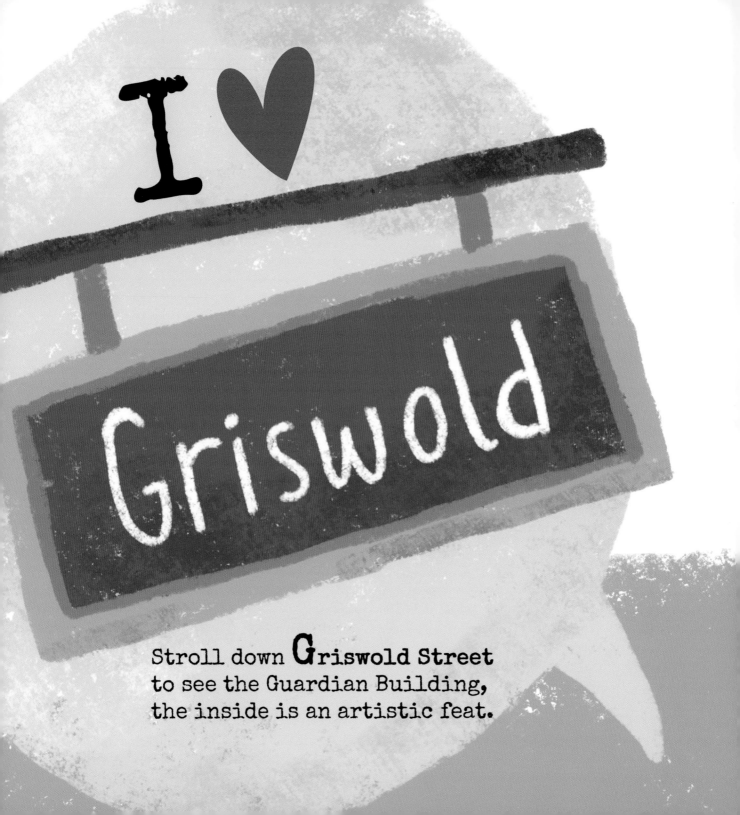

I ♥ Griswold

Stroll down **Griswold Street** to see the Guardian Building, the inside is an artistic feat.

DETROIT HISTORICAL MUSEUM

The **Detroit Historical Museum** bursts with history,
the streets of old Detroit, fur traders
and model trains all tell a story.

Want to see a Picasso?

The **Detroit Institute of Arts**
also has murals and art by Van Gogh!

We wear our Detroit **j**erseys proud.
For our Tigers, Lions, Pistons and Red Wings
we cheer so loud!

Albert Kahn designed the **Kales Building** with glory.
First offices, now beautiful homes fill each story.

The **Detroit Public Library** has more than a great book,
from mosaics to painted windows, come have a look!

Motown Museum was first a music studio,
hit songs were recorded here
before being played on the radio.

Jam to live music at New Center Park, or watch an outdoor movie after dark.

Oh! Campus Martius Park is the place to be!
In summer play at the beach and fountains,
in winter go skating and see a giant Christmas tree!

Take a tour at **P**ewabic Pottery,
famous for its iridescent glazes.
A historic landmark is its gallery.

Up above the streets so high,
the People Mover travels in the sky.

The **Q**Line streetcars
travel around,
the city streets
upon the ground.

The seven towers of the **R**en **C**en shine,
forever a part of the Detroit skyline.

The **S**pirit of Detroit is a famous statue.
In his left he holds a sphere for the Father,
in his right a family that includes me and you.

The **Detroit Masonic** Temple is the largest of its kind,
built with Gothic architecture that's really hard to find.

Learn about the Earth, Moon and Mars

at Wayne State University Planetarium,
and see a night sky full of stars.

Head to the **V**elodrome for biking inside,
around and around the oval track you'll ride!

Woodward Avenue angles from south to north.
Here, parades and classic cars put their best forth.

Looking for a delicious, thick & crunchy treat?

Some e**X**cellent Detroit style pizza you should eat!

In 1701 the French explorers landed here,

and in 2001 Detroit celebrated its 300th **y**ear!

DETROIT ZOO

The **Detroit Zoo** in Royal Oak
is home to penguins, tigers and giraffes.
Visit the fountains for a splash or soak!

I is for Inspiration.
For Cat and Boy, who inspired these rhymes.
We always have the best of times.
XO Mama

G is for Grateful.
I am grateful to all my family and friends
who read early versions of this book!
Thank you so much for taking a look!
Forrest
Trisha Kay
Allison
Stephanie
& Mindy

www.GreenMittenMama.com

Learn more about the author,
find FREE coloring page downloads
and shop more ABCDetroit products!

Design Your Own Spirit of Detroit!

I want to see your design! Send me your colored picture at
KariJo@GreenMittenMama.com to be featured online.

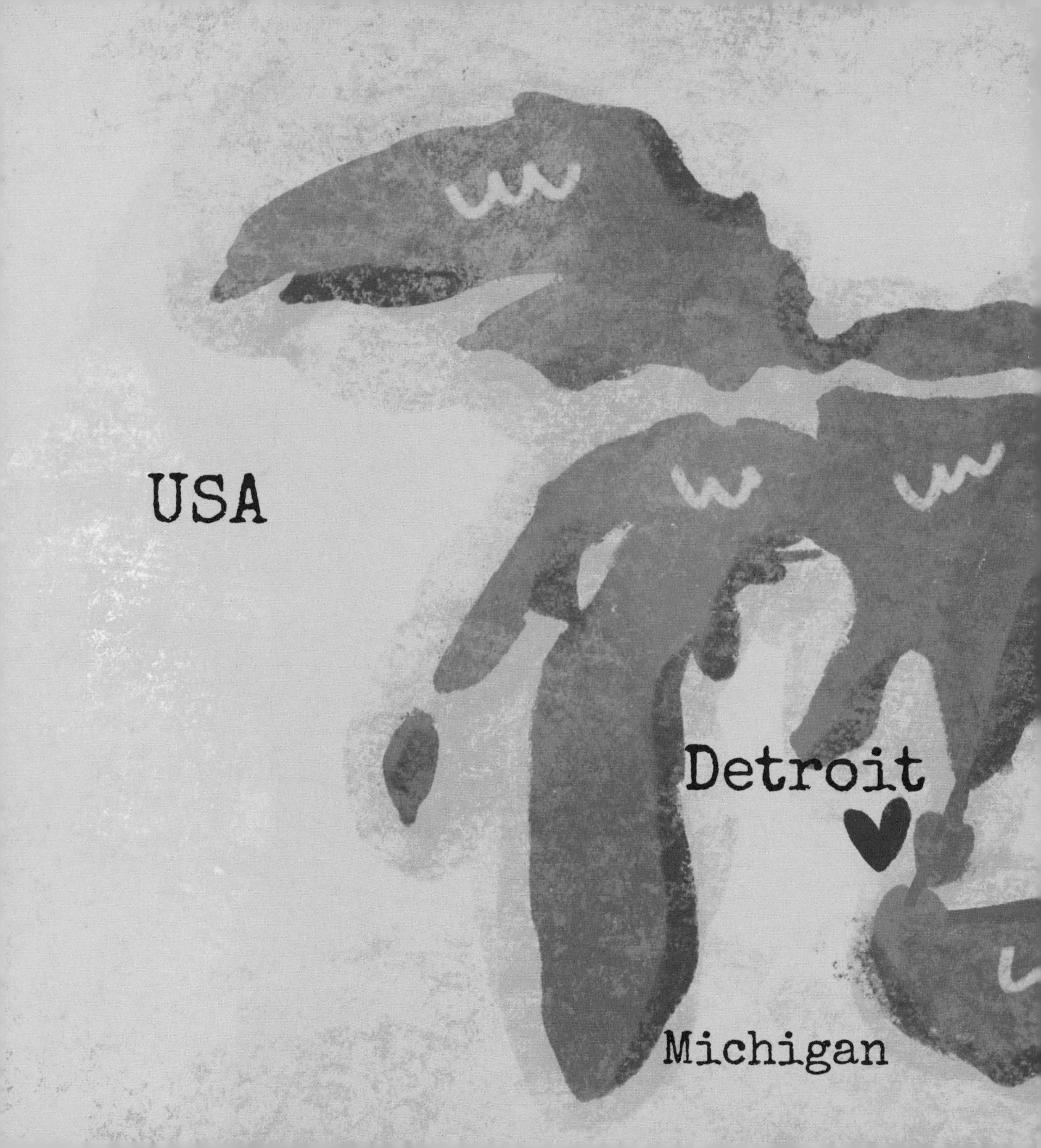
USA
Detroit
Michigan